Newcastle
City Council

Newcastle Libraries and Information Service

☎ **0191 277 4100**

19/1/15.

Please return this item to any of Newcastle's Libraries by the last date shown above. If not requested by another customer the loan can be renewed, you can do this by phone, post or in person.

Charges may be made for late returns.

A Reel Meaning for
Christmas

By Carol Foote

Finding Yourself in
the Classic
Christmas Films

Pleasant Word
A Division of WINEPRESS PUBLISHING

Pleasant Word (a division of WinePress Publishing, PO Box 428, Enumclaw, WA 98022) functions only as book publisher. As such, the ultimate design, content, editorial accuracy, and views expressed or implied in this work are those of the author.

Scripture references marked NKJV are taken from the New King James Version, © 1979, 1980, 1982 by Thomas Nelson, Inc., Publishers. Used by permission.

Scripture references marked NLT are taken from the Holy Bible, New Living Translation, copyright © 1996 by Tyndale Charitable Trust. Used by permission of Tyndale House Publishers, Wheaton, Illinois 60189. All rights reserved.

Order Ref: KOB90293

Caption and Credit Information for The Kobal Collection

Title: WHITE CHRISTMAS
Pers: VERA-ELLEN CLOONEY, ROSEMARY
Year: 1954
Dir: CURTIZ, MICHAEL
Ref: WHI001AV
Credit: [PARAMOUNT / THE KOBAL COLLECTION]

Title: PREACHER'S WIFE, THE
Pers: HOUSTON, WHITNEY WASHINGTON, DENZEL
Year: 1996
Dir: MARSHALL, PENNY
Ref: PRE048AE
Credit: [TOUCHSTONE / THE KOBAL COLLECTION / LEE, DAVID]

Title: IT'S A WONDERFUL LIFE
Pers: STEWART, JAMES REED, DONNA
Year: 1946
Dir: CAPRA, FRANK
Ref: ITS006AQ
Credit: [RKO / THE KOBAL COLLECTION]

Title: GRAHAME, GLORIA
Pers: GRAHAME, GLORIA
Year: 1946
Ref: XGR003AI
Credit: [MGM / THE KOBAL COLLECTION]

Title: YOUNG, LORETTA
Pers: YOUNG, LORETTA
Ref: XYO002DR
Credit: [THE KOBAL COLLECTION]

Title: CHRISTMAS IN CONNECTICUT
Pers: STANWYCK, BARBARA MORGAN, DENNIS
Year: 1945
Dir: GODFREY, PETER
Ref: CHR008AA
Credit: [UNIVERSAL / THE KOBAL COLLECTION / JULIAN, MAC]

Bensen Music: "All I Ever Have To Be" by Gary W. Chapman © 1980 Paragon Corp.

The Christine Ward Literary Agency: Excerpt from "The Art of Speed Reading People", by Paul D. Tieger and Barbara Barron-Tieger © 1998, reprinted by permission.

ISBN 13: 978-1-4141-0552-9
ISBN 10: 1-4141-0552-5
Library of Congress Catalog Card Number: 2005907961

This book is dedicated to;

Bud, Norma, Barb, Al, Audrey, Tom, and Kate
who watched these movies with me,
my husband and kids who insisted I complete this project,
my parents who generously contributed to secure these pictures
Darren and Dannette who diligently worked to prepare the layout
and to my aunt, who does a good job of living the
life-style characterized by these leading ladies.

Table of Contents

Acknowledgments

Scripture references are from the New Living Translation (NLT) and The New King James Version. (NKJV)

Screen Test Selected Questions and Analysis are taken from:

The Art of SpeedReading People. Little, Brown and Company, Boston, 1998.

1. References regarding the original language for the text from John 4:46-53 are from Spirit-tone Scripture Meditations. "The Timing of Faith John 4:46-53." www.spirittone.com /meditations.
2. References regarding Jesus' fulfillment of 300 Old Testament prophecies are taken from Goring, Bill. "Prophecy As a Proof of Bible Inspiration." 19th Annual Mid-West Lectures, 2001.
3. References for the commentary on Psalm 15 are taken from Stowell, Joseph. "Proclaim! Transcripts." May 12-16 2003.
4. References to the song, *All I Ever Have to Be* are taken from Grant, Amy. Word Records, 1980.

Lights

"The world changes, but two things remain constant—Youth and Beauty."

That's some intriguing statement, considering the speaker is an angel—a Christmas angel played by Cary Grant. Whether speaking as a celestial authority, or just speaking as himself, there is eternal truth in that line. But maybe not at face value. At face value, we may misinterpret its simplicity and pursue both youth and beauty through cosmetic means. As consumers of pop culture, we've been practically brainwashed into thinking that a cosmetic upgrade is *the* catalyst to increased self-esteem. But if we are still thinking, we're well aware that any lasting improvements in self-esteem start on the inside and have everything to do with choosing and controlling our perspectives and values.

If you are as much a fan of classic cinema as you are of pop culture, you recognize the timelessness of a great story and the lasting qualities of a memorable character. Nowhere else is this more evident than in the classic Christmas films. In these films, our favorite characters live out their entire existence in the space of two hours. Yet we resurrect them season after season as we faithfully re-rent, re-watch and rewind them. We *know* these characters. We can anticipate what they'll do, we know what they'll say, and we love them because we identify with them. We have experienced the same doubts and disappointments, and we share some of the same aspirations, virtues and character traits.

Now this implies that these characters are worthy to be role models, and that we should be flattered if we find out we're like them. Well, who wouldn't want to be like them? Collectively they are beautiful, charming, enduring and eventually triumphant. (Some of them even have incredibly small waists.) Actually, in each of these ladies lie the same faults and imperfections that we would like to subdue in our own characters. Though these characters don't even exist in reality, hypothetically they represent the best and worst of us. By virtue of the drama, the best of them is triumphant in the end. They are our heroes. We love these characters because we love their *character*. Their *character* is what keeps them eternally young and beautiful despite the changes in culture. Developing our own character will keep us young and beautiful longer than any cosmetic we could ever apply.

In order to give another perspective on character development, Christian tradition asserts that God equips us with special traits, which mirror His own character and are also seen in His Son, Jesus Christ. Because we are unable to attain these by ourselves, some of these virtues were genetically transferred onto the DNA of our souls when we were made in God's image. In Latin, this is known as the *Imago Dei* the very likeness and presence of God in each of us. Other virtues develop as we observe role models, both real and fictitious, living out these traits in their daily dramas.

That's how we get movie heroes in the first place. Hopefully we also have some real live heroes upon which to model our lives. Modern western history defines Jesus Christ as a hero worth modeling. The tragic combination of original sin (Eve and Adam's fall), accompanied by our own perpetual preferences for ourselves over God, contributed to the fading of Imago Dei and initially broke our connection with God. Jesus, who is God in a human form, had to first be born in order to die sacrificially for our sins. And that's what Christmas is all about. Now, here's the Good News! Scripture suggests that the remnant of *Imago Dei* sparks our passion to connect with our Creator. Once we find out that the powerful possibility of reconciliation and re-connection **is available**, we will long to get to know our Creator better. As we learn more things about His character, we discover that these are the same character traits we have admired in others and long to develop and perfect within ourselves. It seems that was God's original plan when He first made us in His image. With this in mind, it may require a paradigm shift in our thinking, but it should not be a surprise to conclude the following:

1. God made us in His image so that we could connect with Him, and share something in common with Him, so
2. He could enjoy a relationship with His creation at His level.

Simply stated, the way we get to have a personal relationship with God, and really get to know Him intimately, is to have a relationship with Jesus Christ. The most important questions we will ever ask ourselves are:

• Do we know Jesus Christ?
• How can we get to know Him better?

A relationship with Him will provide a makeover from the inside out. With His influence, we can develop those beautiful and enduring character traits we admire in our heroes and heroines. Even Billy Graham says that the most "Extreme Makeover" we'll ever have is when we let Jesus be Lord of our lives.

The original intent of this project was to encourage self-esteem in women by reintroducing them to some well-loved role models with whom they could identify. Because I had long loved these same ladies, I knew what it was like to identify with them. Throughout some of my formative years, and even into early adulthood, I had tried at times to look, act or talk like them.

Drawing lines from these classic movies, I would quote something witty or poignant into conversations to see if I got any reactions. At times, people with a similar nostalgia would respond with a quote. More often than not, my family and friends would just smile. If I felt good recreating these little vignettes, my idea was to affirm contemporary women by acknowledging that they share some enduring values and virtues with their on-screen heroes. As I continued to write, it seemed God was saying to me, "Why do you just want to be like them, when you can be like Me?" It was not until I agreed to describe and inject the source of all goodness into the text that I experienced any peace about the project, or the sparks of enthusiasm that came from recalling the Scriptures and anecdotes used in this work. So, while it is thoroughly natural and appropriate to have movie role models to admire for their virtues, it is so much more important that we recognize God to be the author and supplier of those characteristics in the first place.

While writing this, these words from songwriter Amy Grant replayed inside my head.

"And I realize the good in me is only there
Because of who You are,
And all I ever have to be is what you made me."
Amy Grant *All I Ever Have to Be* 1980 WORD, Inc.

Those of us who love these old films then can rest assured that our attraction to them is from God, and when viewed appropriately, they can bring us into an even more intimate relationship with Him at this most significant time of year. This book is meant to be shared with friends who need to be introduced to their creator for the first time. For those of us who know Him, it can also serve as a daily resource for meditations on the indescribable and vast goodness of our creator.

Participating in the "Screen Test" will connect you with the personality of a well-known character associated with a classic Christmas film. The first group of characters demonstrates the seeking, teachable heart that is essential to respond to God's invitations of intimacy. The second group of characters displays some of the virtues that are perfected in the person of God Himself. In making these comparisons, I do not take the character of God lightly. My intent is to select characters who are often associated with Christmas, then draw some comparisons between them and the original author of Christmas. When you identify your companion character, you will receive a personally applicable synopsis of the movie along with related Scripture for follow-up study.

This book is intended to be read interactively. After reading the introduction and taking the screen test, please locate and read about your companion character. Refer to the screen test and analysis again before reading about a second character.

Screen Test ❧

FIND OUT WHERE YOU FIT INTO
YOUR FAVORITE CHRISTMAS FILMS

TAKE THE SCREEN TEST!
COMPARE YOUR PERSONALITY WITH
THE FAMOUS FACES OF THESE FABULOUS FILMS.

When taking the SCREEN TEST, answer each question as automatically as possible. Consider your first reaction to the question rather than spending a long time deliberating over your answer. When you have completed each section, tally up the answers. Don't worry if you have a combination of letters in your answers. If one letter is more prevalent, your personality leans toward that particular trait.

SCREEN TEST

SECTION ONE: Describes how you perceive your world.

These answers will tell you if you rely more heavily on your intuition ("N" answers), or if you learn best through your experiences and senses ("S" answers). Either response is acceptable. The combination of responses contributes to your individuality.

People say I am mostly down to earth and sensible.	S
People say I am mostly imaginative and creative.	N
I am determined to experience the present moment to its fullest.	S
I am concerned about how each of my decisions will affect the future.	N
I am most comfortable to trust my direct experiences.	S
I am most comfortable when I trust my gut instinct.	N

SECTION TWO: How you make your decisions.

When faced with a decision, are you more of a Thinker ("T" answers), or a Feeler ("F" answers)? Either response is viable. The combination of responses contributes to your individuality.

When I make decisions, I write down and compare the pros and cons of the idea.	T
I make my decision based on how I feel at the moment.	F
I am usually more logical and analytical.	T
I am usually more sensitive and **empathetic**	F
I value the importance of truth, even if it hurts someone's feelings.	T
It is more important to be tactful, even if that means telling a little white lie.	F
I am often persuaded by a good logical argument	T
I am often persuaded by a strong emotional appeal	F
I'd rather be complimented for being tough.	T
I'd rather be complimented for being tender.	F

COMPARE YOUR PROFILE SCORES
WITH THE
LEADING LADIES BELOW

If you have a combination of S and F answers you are a Sensor Feeler	If you have a combination of N and F answers you are an Intuitive Feeler
The test analysis shows that 'Sensor Feelers' tend to idealize whomever they admire. They go out of their way to do something helpful and nice for others. Their idea of helping is to assist in real and practical ways. They often find themselves cooperating with others' plans and schemes in order to achieve this. Because they value harmony, they sometimes allow others to influence their own decisions.	'Intuitive Feelers' are just that: patient, insightful, empathetic and perceptive. Their visions and values are top priority for them. They will subject themselves to criticism and skepticism to hold fast to their dreams. Because of this unshakable faith they are inspirational to others. NFs are oriented to the future and express themselves figuratively.
Some words which describe SF: Warm, Friendly, Optimistic, Nostalgic, Diplomatic, Agreeable. Able to juggle several activities at once. They're real and share easily. Others like to be around them.	*Words that best describe the NF:* Spontaneous and Creative. Agreeable and Sociable. May appear emotional. Impulsive and Energetic.
Leading Ladies with S and F personalities include: Mary Bailey-*It's a Wonderful Life* Elizabeth Lane-*Christmas in Connecticut*	Leading Ladies with N and F personalities include: Julia Brougham-*The Bishop's Wife* Violet Bick–*It's a Wonderful Life* Judy Haines-*White Christmas*

If you have a combination of S and T answers you are a Sensor Thinker	If you have a combination of N and T answers you are an Intuitive Thinker
Sensor Thinkers are logical, objective and analytical. They are most confident making decisions based upon past experiences. They are known to be calm in a crisis and able to suppress their emotional reactions during such times. Because they have learned this control, they tend to think of their emotional and social life as being less important as other aspects of life. Persuaded only by logical appeals, they are good listeners and are comfortable with thinking through their ideas before acting on them.	Intuitive Thinkers have a knack for looking at things and seeing how they can be improved. While they can easily imagine improvements and possibilities in things, their favorite subject for improvement is themselves. They are on a constant quest for knowledge, setting high standards for themselves and others. A logical persuasion appeals to the NT who thinks it's fun to make their point clear.
Some adjectives for ST personalities: Private, Trustworthy. Oriented to the present. Loyal, Confident, Thorough. ST's are natural leaders and their friends ask them for advice often.	*Adjectives that best describe the NT:* Ingenious, Imaginative. Creative, Innovative.
Leading Ladies with S and T personalities: * Betty Haines–*White Christmas* * Doris Walker–*Miracle on 34th Street*	*Leading Ladies with N and T personalities:* * Julia Biggs–*The Preacher's Wife*

The above questions and analyses are taken from:

Tieger, Paul and Barron-Tieger, Barbara. *The Art of SpeedReading People.* Little, Brown and Company, Boston. 1998.

Camera

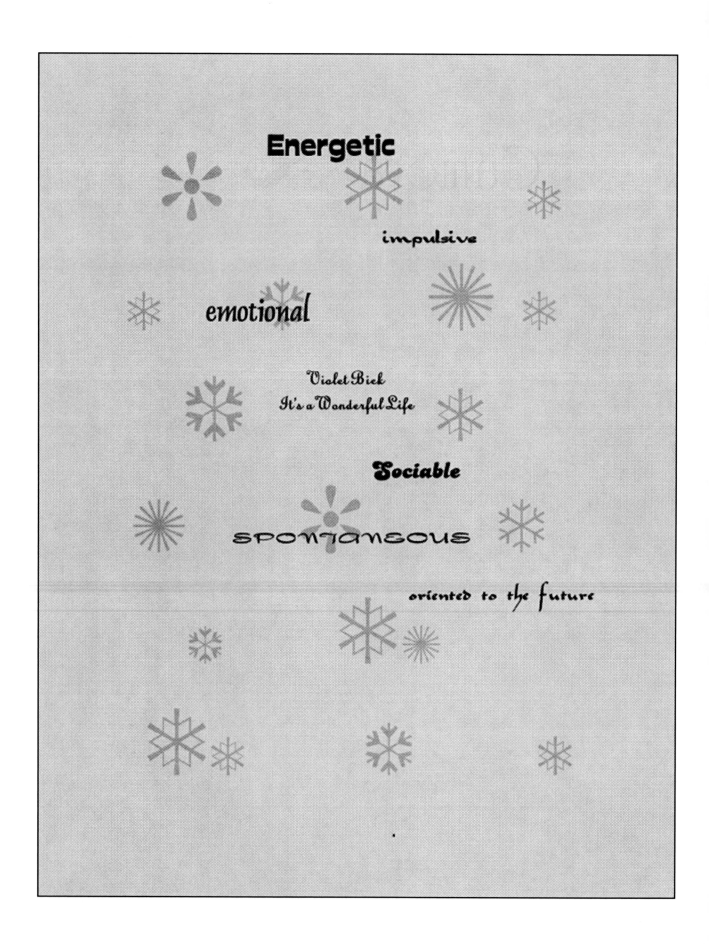

Energetic

impulsive

emotional

Violet Bick
It's a Wonderful Life

Sociable

spontaneous

oriented to the future

VIOLET BICK
IN
IT'S A WONDERFUL LIFE

"Excuse Me! I think I got a date! But stick around fellas-just in case!"

Violet Bick is essential in making Bedford Falls feel like a real place. Every town (every high school, every office) has someone like her. Flirty, optimistic and determined to have fun, Violet is very busy controlling the circumstances to ensure that outcome. All of this doesn't preclude her from asking for help when she needs it–and she knows exactly who to go to for that help. Violet is confident enough in George Bailey to know that he won't turn her aside, even when her intentions are to use his help for her own purposes yet again.

God will never turn away a genuine seeker. He loves to show Himself faithful to those who need to learn to trust Him. Each time our heavenly Father comes to the rescue, along with appreciation, another logical response should be a little more confidence that God is who He says He is. (He says it all in the Bible. A good place to start is the gospel of John.)

The book of John is filled with real stories of real people seeking Jesus. A nobleman from Judea had a son who was sick to the point of death. (John 4:46-53). He desperately sought Jesus to help him in this emergency. Apparently this man was aware of Jesus' reputation and ability to heal, for he came from another part of Israel to where Jesus was staying. He had to ask Jesus twice to heal his son because he did not get the initial response that he expected. Upon begging Jesus to intervene, Jesus instructed the man to go home for his son would live. The Bible reports that the man believed Jesus and went his way.

Upon his journey home, the nobleman met up with his servants who reported that a miracle healing had occurred at the very time when he was seeking the Lord. The Bible specifically states *again* that the man believed, only this time his whole household believed along with him.

An interesting fact related to this is the original language used for the two words translated into "believe." The word *believe,* as used in verse 50, describes a skeptical desperation to believe as a last resort in an emergency situation. Spirit-tone Commentary states, "What brought this man to (Jesus) was hope, or probably what he felt was his last hope."

The word *believe,* as used in vs. 53, depicts a confidence that comes from having a relationship with the one who can make good on His promises to us. What started as a last hope and became belief in a promise grew into an all-consuming belief in the Son of God. It didn't take long for this seeking nobleman to experience a confident belief in Jesus that eventually connected to his entire household. Because of one man's enounter with the Lord, an entire household was changed.

This experiential, confident belief is the kind that resulted in real connection and relationship for Violet Bick. It is a less impulsive Violet who returns the money to George on Christmas Eve. Now more reflective, her plans for leaving Bedford Falls have changed. Her revised plans include staying put and staying connected to the hometown in which she has always belonged.

When all of our searching leads us back to the plans that God has for us, we will be connected, and we will be home.

Yo

This Christmas get to know the real reason for the season–Jesus Christ.
He would die for you to get to know him.

GREAT QUOTES FROM
IT'S A WONDERFUL LIFE

"Excuse Me! I think I got a date! But stick around fellas just in case!!"

SOME GREAT QUOTES FROM GOD
ABOUT HOW TO SEEK AND FIND HIM

"Those who know your name trust in you, for you, O Lord, have never abandoned anyone who searches for you."

—Psalm 9:10 NLT

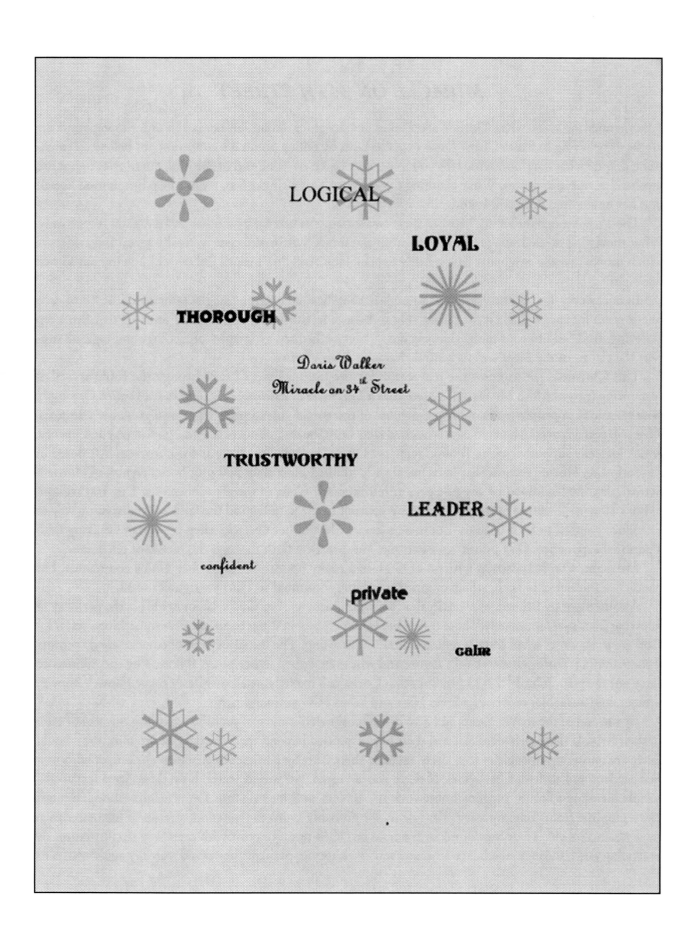

LOGICAL

LOYAL

THOROUGH

Doris Walker
Miracle on 34th Street

TRUSTWORTHY

LEADER

confident

private

calm

DORIS WALKER
IN
MIRACLE ON 34TH STREET

Remember the scene when Doris Walker takes her daughter, Susan, on her lap in order to expound the merits of believing in Santa Claus? Doris explains faith by telling Susan it's continuing to believe in something despite what common sense tells you to believe. Later, near the end of the film, Susan tries to put her mother's advice into action. While claiming to believe in Kris Kringle, Susan can't help but remind herself that her new-found faith still sounds silly.

There's not much difference between these two statements uttered by mother and daughter respectively. What these girls needed was proof. It takes until the movie's ultimate scene to finally reveal the evidence, which proves that the enigmatic Kris is really Santa Claus. And don't we all feel better knowing our hunch was right?

In our twenty-first century religious smorgasbord (where all religions are the same so a little bit of each one is good for me, right?), it may seem silly to believe in the exclusive claims of Jesus Christ. But keep believing. And "add to your faith... knowledge..." because history, geography, archeology and logic all support the claims of the Bible and its central character Jesus Christ.

This Christmas get to know the real reason for the season–Jesus Christ–through the Bible as well as supporting texts like Josh Mc Dowell's *More than a Carpenter* or *Evidence that Demands a Verdict*. Or simply pose questions to people whose faith and defense of the gospel you admire. When you go to these sources, what will you discover? Meticulously researched facts from the disciplines of science, philosophy and history, which logically support ancient, Biblical references regarding people, places and occurrences first noted in the Scripture. History records that Jesus has already fulfilled more than 300 prophecies regarding Himself. Statistically, the likelihood of any one person fulfilling any eight of those prophecies is 1 in 100 trillion. (That's 10 with 40 zeroes behind it.) Steeping yourself in the facts behind the faith is an intriguing way to introduce yourself to faith in Jesus. But there's frequently another obstacle when it comes to making faith a personal experience. God prioritizes a personal and practical faith through the means of obedience.

Abraham, who is known as a friend of God, had many opportunities to obey God's commands. His obedience translated to faith, which eventually became accounted to Him for righteousness.

A contemporary believer may testify that her willingness to obey God's call in her life is the pathway to knowing Jesus more intimately. Those times that we experience inklings to accomplish something special for God are those times when Jesus is telling us to do something. The initial steps to obedience are discerning if these inklings correspond to God's nature and will as described in Scripture, followed by the mindset to carry out the plan. John 14:21-23 promises that Christ will make Himself manifest (make Himself known, present, and available) to whoever loves Him and keeps His commandments.

By the end of the movie, Doris and Susan Walker showed some real promise regarding the area of faith in their lives. If these girls were real and their lives extended beyond the boundary of the film, they would likely encounter opportunities to actively increase their faith by participating in new challenges with new perspectives and different behaviors. If there was a sequel, we would watch how these "two lost souls" handle blending a family, juggling housework and careers, and moving into a new neighborhood. Sounds like a plot line from contemporary prime time. *We* probably know the potential stresses of life better than these characters did. Their newfound faith would be called upon to grow with each new circumstance. By practicing faith, through obedience to a new way of thinking, perhaps they could one day agree with Kris

Kringle's effective philosophy that "Christmas isn't just a day—It's a frame of mind." But for now let me encourage you:

This Christmas get to know the real reason for the season—Jesus Christ
(along with all the peace and perspective that His presence will bring to you).

He'd die for you to get to know Him.

MIRACLE ON 34TH STREET

(Sorry, picture and quote are not available.
You should probably just watch the film.)

FAVORITE QUOTES FROM THE BIBLE REGARDING FAITH

" Then add to your faith virtue, and to virtue knowledge, and to knowledge self control..."

—2 Peter 1:5 NKJV

" So Abraham believed God, and it was accounted to him as righteousness."

—James 2:23 NKJV

"What is faith? It is the confident assurance that what we hope for is going to happen. It is the evidence of things we cannot yet see."

—Hebrews 11:1 NLT

"The just shall live by faith."

—Romans 1:17 NKJV

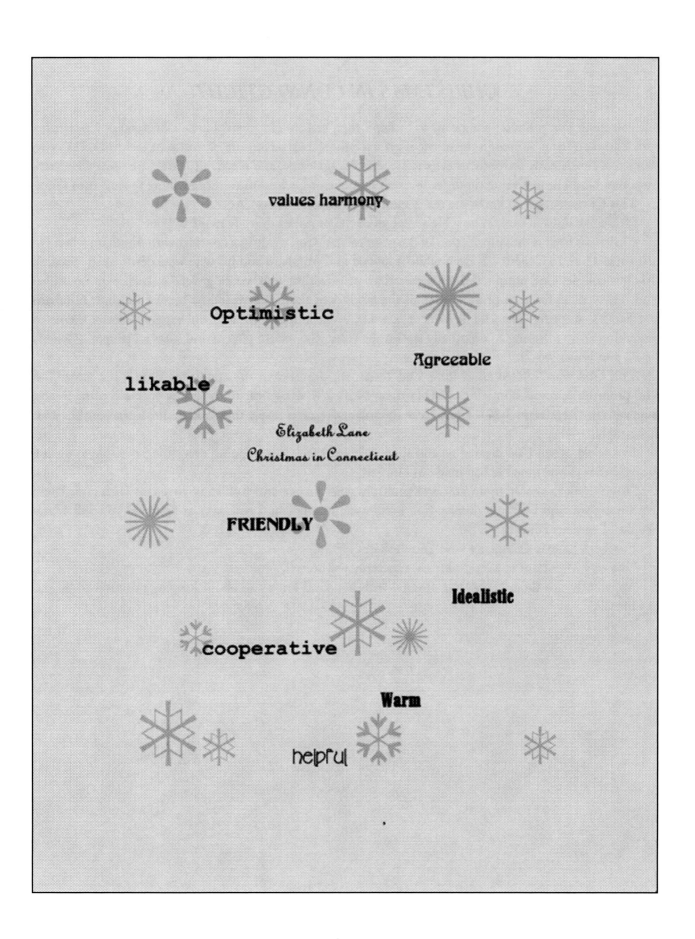

values harmony

Optimistic

Agreeable

likable

Elizabeth Lane
Christmas in Connecticut

FRIENDLY

Idealistic

cooperative

Warm

helpful

ELIZABETH LANE
IN
CHRISTMAS IN CONNECTICUT

If you think that promises are meant to be kept, then you should spend a little *Christmas in Connecticut* with Elizabeth Lane. Although the movie itself is a lighthearted adventure of mistaken identities, Liz's two characters consistently prove themselves to be reliable, agreeable, and teachable. These are some characteristics that God Himself values in order to teach permanent life lessons to those willing to tune into Him.

This Christmas get to know the real reason for the season–Jesus Christ.

He's so anxious to explain how He's kept all of the promises that He made to you.

Christmas itself is the culmination of the promise that God made in a contract with Abraham when He first sought him in Genesis 12. Even while it looked as if Abraham and his wife were destined to remain a childless couple, God promised them generations of offspring who would govern in their own bountiful land. He went so far as to promise that all the families of the Earth would be blessed through Abraham and Sarah's offspring. The Old Testament is a 4,000-year odyssey with an unchanging central theme of preserving these offspring to eventually spawn the ruler who would govern and bless all people. (Genesis 12-22 and Isaiah 9:6-7).

This God who fulfilled all of these Old Testament promises at the appointed time is the same God who promises to reveal Himself to us (Matthew 14:21-23), draw near to us (James 4:8) and come in and dine with us (Revelation 3:20). These New Testament promises imply that God desires a relationship with His people.

In a sense, when God created us and then redeemed us, He was doing everything possible to keep a promise that at one time He had made to Himself.

"I will look favorably upon you and multiply your people and fulfill my covenant with you. I will live among you and I will not despise you. I will walk among you; I will be your God and you will be my people." Leviticus 26: 9-12

Elizabeth Lane is a character who knows that:

"It's very important to keep promises–especially to yourself."

Apparently this thought was not original with her. God knows all about keeping promises to us and to Himself.

A QUOTE FROM
CHRISTMAS IN CONNECTICUT

"It's very important to keep promises–especially to yourself."

SOME OF GOD'S FAVORITE PROMISES

"I will walk among you, I will be your God and you will be My people."

—Leviticus 26:12 NKJV

"For you are a holy people, who belong to the Lord your God. Of all the people on earth, the Lord your God has chosen you to be his own special treasure."

—Deuteronomy 7:6 NKJV

"For all of God's promises have been fulfilled in (Jesus Christ)."

—2 Corinthians 1:20 NLT

"This is the promise that He has promised us–Eternal Life."

—1 John 2:25 NKJV

"We know that all things work together for good, for those who love God…"

—Romans 8:28 NKJV

Intermission ❧ and Academy Awards

When we are first introduced to Jesus, our relationship with Him will be successful, or not, solely based upon the condition of our heart. Chuck Colson talks much about the vulnerability of *Imago Dei*. Apparently, if we neglect and deny it too often it will fade and be hard to recapture. The previous leading ladies responded to the opportunities in their movies with seeking and teachable hearts. They are our heroes because they faced their moment of destiny and changed for the better. They connected with their *Imago Dei* and they were rewarded with second chances and new opportunities. While you may hate to see your favorite movies end, have you ever contemplated sequels to these classics? No doubt our heroines would have to face challenges that required them to use and practice their new-found faith. A lot of them got married. Enough said.

On the other hand, this next group of ladies seems to have established portions of their *Imago Dei* early on. (Can we imagine their life before the movie?) Their particular strengths were reliable enough to withstand the inevitable crises of the drama. They are our heroes because they are consistent. They have one or two virtuous characteristics down pat enough to succeed in helping others, but how does their *Imago Dei* rate when it's compared with a standard? Perhaps we should be careful here. As mentioned in the introduction, I do not take God's holiness lightly. Obviously no one can compare with God's standard of holiness and perfection. But if we're honest with ourselves, sometimes we'd have to admit that we're content with basking in our abilities and gifts, assuming at times that our goodness is good enough. Let's look at how God speaks about the level of His standards.

PSALM 15

Who can abide in Your tabernacle?
Who can dwell in Your holy hill? NKJV

After asking rhetorical questions about the eligibility for intimacy with God, Psalm 15 records a list of the character qualifications necessary for such a relationship. The people eligible to abide in God's tabernacle and dwell on His holy hill all have the following characteristics. Let's see how our leading ladies measure up.

<u>Those who live blameless lives.</u> (verse 2). No nominations here. Even Mary Bailey can't qualify for this award. But God is a God of uprightness, integrity and righteousness. God is who He says He is. He is holy, and there is no unrighteousness or hypocrisy in Him.

<u>Those who speak the truth from sincere hearts and refuse to slander, harm, or speak evil of neighbors and friends</u> (verses 2-3). Probably all of our ladies could be nominated for this category, but the winner

is Betty Haines from *White Christmas.* She does a great job of speaking forthrightly. No angles or hidden agendas for her. Betty's only problem is that she jumps to conclusions. Her assumptions cause her to make decisions before she has all the information. But God is a God of truth and transparency. He will never slander or speak ill of us. When He thinks of us, He is thinking about how much He loves us. He says that His love covers a multitude of sins, and that when we confess them, He forgets about them. He will never bring them up to us again. When commenting on this Psalm, Moody Bible Institute's President Joseph Stowell describes God as a good "…neighbor, because He came from a different neighborhood to our neighborhood to love us to the Cross…"

Those who honor the faithful followers of the Lord (verse 4). And the nominees are…Julia Brougham and Julia Biggs. Both married to men of the cloth, these Julias are committed to their husbands and the lifestyles that result from such a sacrifice. Although they never do anything technically wrong, they are often angry. They can't look past their particular circumstances to really enjoy the Christmas season without some supernatural assistance. On the other hand, God honors and befriends those who fear Him (Psalm 25:14).

Those who keep their promises when it hurts (verse 4). Here's another nomination for both Julias, the bishop's and the preacher's wives. They remained faithful to their husbands even when tempted by happier and more carefree relationships. Judy Haines is also a nominee. She goes through an awful lot of trouble to remain a devoted sister. The winner, though, is Mary Bailey. She made a promise to love George Bailey forever—even if George never heard it—because she whispered it into his bad ear in Gower's drugstore back when they were kids. Mary spent her life keeping that promise in her unmistakably cheerful way. Assuming that her wedding vows included "for richer for poorer," she had the opportunity to make good on both those counts. Our God prioritizes keeping His promises. The promises that He made to Abraham and Sarah in Genesis finally became possible 4,000 years later at the birth of Jesus. Those promises are still being fulfilled today, for we are of the blessed generations that He promised to Abraham and his wife way back then.

Those who do not charge interest on the money they lend, nor take bribes against the innocent. Yes, the Bible says this in Psalm 15:5. Interestingly, this very topic arises with the Bailey's as well as with Elizabeth Lane. They are generous to lend, and likely to forfeit any interest when necessary, but they are in business to make a living. I'm confident that God is not discouraging us from making an honest living as much as He is demonstrating that His generosity far exceeds our own. He owns everything in the world, and He gives generously to all men.

From this Psalm, we can make some important observations. While our leading ladies fit nicely into a few of these categories, they are clearly unable to qualify for them all. The point being none of us will ever be completely eligible on our own to equal a perfection that is not humanly possible. But that's not completely bad news. After some study and reflection, another observation becomes clear. This list of things that humans will never achieve is also a list of things that God already is. Stowell goes on to explain,

> "Why does God want us to be like this list? Because that's what He is. That's where He is. That's when you start sharing some things in common. Therefore, you begin to experience fellowship. It's commonality. You know, it's kind of like moving in with God. He doesn't do bitterness, and He doesn't do revenge, and He doesn't do cheating and lying… It's a matter of commonality. It's getting to be where God is. And the wonderful thing is it's not hard to get across the border. You don't have to have a passport or visa. The Cross is the visa and the passport to get into His territory."

So now I finally offer up this last group of characters as role models. Imperfect, like us they have not perfected *Imago Dei.* But because they are practicing behaviors that will nurture *Imago Dei,* their lives portray some of the virtues to which we aspire. Aristotle says that we acquire the virtues the same way we acquire a habit. If we would habitually put into practice our *Imago Dei* virtues as often as we watch these films, there is the possibility for an eternal, extreme makeover in our own lives.

values harmony

Optimistic

Agreeable

likable

Mary Bailey
It's a Wonderful Life

FRIENDLY

Nostalgic

cooperative

Warm

Sharing

MARY BAILEY
IN
IT'S A WONDERFUL LIFE

"You see, George, you really had a wonderful life."

Perhaps it is more appropriate for our purposes to say, "...you really had a wonderful wife." But George Bailey already knew that. Try as he might, he couldn't resist Mary Hatch. Even though he wanted to "shake off the dust of this crummy little town," deep down he loved the friendly, popular, nostalgic girl who admired him and wanted to go out of her way to make for him a home.

When someone admires those traits of loyalty, sympathy, graciousness, and idealism in others, it is likely that they find a bit of those characteristics within themselves.

It's no coincidence that you share these positive qualities or admire their presence in others. Your own creator designed you with these traits because He is

loyal

sympathetic and **empathetic**

gracious and

idealistic Himself.

This Christmas get to know the real reason for the season—Jesus Christ.
He would die for you to get to know Him.

THE BEST QUOTES FROM
IT'S A WONDERFUL LIFE

"What is it you want, Mary? You want the moon? Just say the word, and I'll throw a lasso around it and pull it down. Hey—that's a good idea—I'll give you the moon."

"I'll take it—then what?"

THE BEST QUOTES FROM GOD
REGARDING HIS CHARACTER

LOYAL/FAITHFUL

"He is the faithful God who keeps His covenant for a thousand generations, and constantly loves those who love Him."

—Deuteronomy 7:9 NLT

SYMPATHETIC/EMPATHETIC

"We have a High Priest who sympathizes with our weaknesses."

—Hebrews 4:15 NKJV

GRACIOUS

"But You are a God of forgiveness, gracious and merciful, slow to become angry and full of unfailing love and mercy."

—Nehemiah 9:17 NLT

IDEALISTIC

"I know the plans I have for you, says the Lord. They are plans for good and not for disaster, to give you a future and a hope."

—Jeremiah 29:11 NLT

LOGICAL

LOYAL

THOROUGH

Betty Haines
White Christmas

TRUSTWORTHY

LEADER

confident

private

BETTY HAINES
IN
WHITE CHRISTMAS

When you can't sleep, do you count your blessings instead of sheep? If so, you might identify with that realistic, common sense sister–Betty Haines. The girl with the "deep blue" eyes is trustworthy and idealistic. Having the ability to listen more than she talks, she also prioritizes speaking the truth when she does finally open up. Although usually calm under all circumstances, she feels strong emotion in response to the drama in the lives surrounding her own. But we're not fooling ourselves. We know everything's not "…beautiful in Vermont this time of year." Betty has some flaws (just like all of us) that get her into trouble.

But we're just talking about the positive qualities here, and it's not just by chance that you share the virtues listed above. Your own creator designed you with these characteristics, because He is trustworthy, idealistic, truthful, and emotional Himself. Did you ever think you could have something in common with God? After all, He made you in His image in order to have a relationship with you.

This Christmas, get to know the real reason for the season–Jesus Christ.
He would die for you to get to know Him better.

"I know exactly what I'm going to dream about tonight"

GREAT QUOTES FROM THE BIBLE ABOUT GOD'S CHARACTER

TRUSTWORTHY/FAITHFUL

"He is the faithful God who keeps His covenant for a thousand generations, and constantly loves those who love Him."

—Deuteronomy 7:9 NLT

IDEALISTIC

"I know the plans I have for you, says the Lord. They are plans for good and not for disaster, to give you a future and a hope."

—Jeremiah 29:11 NLT

TRUTHFUL

"[My] truth endures to all generations."

—Psalm 100:5 NKJV paraphrased

EMOTIONAL

"We have a High Priest who sympathizes with our weaknesses."

—Hebrews 4:15 NKJV paraphrased

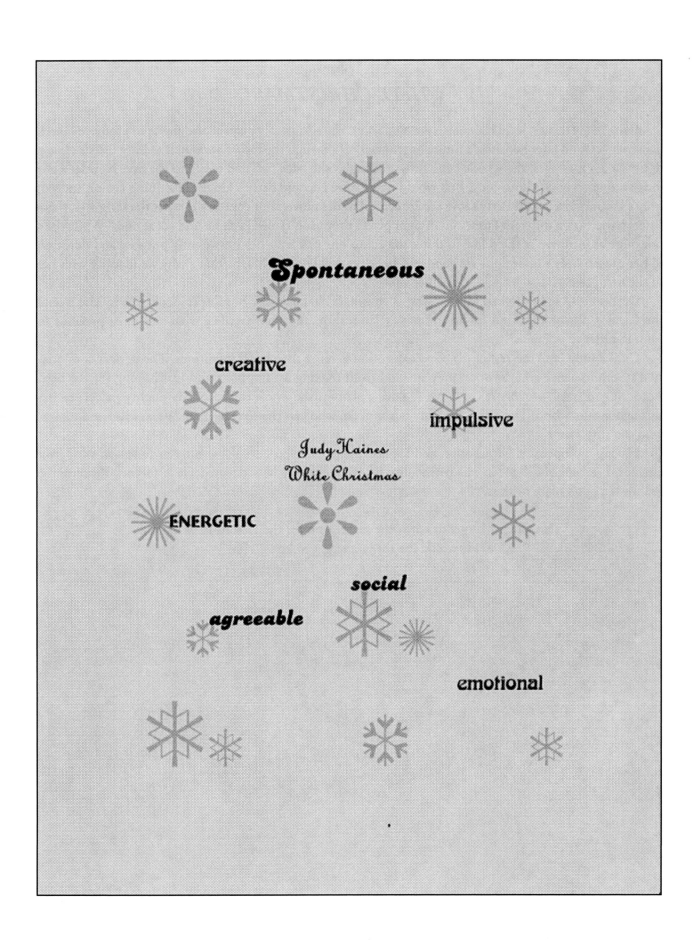

Spontaneous

creative

impulsive

Judy Haines
White Christmas

ENERGETIC

social

agreeable

emotional

JUDY HAINES
IN
WHITE CHRISTMAS

Among many things, Judy Haines is a devoted sister. She admittedly plays all the angles to promote—first, her sister act, and later her sister's future happiness. All through the movie we watch as Judy listens closely to unspoken messages, the wheels constantly turning as she adds two and two…to get five. Now let's not judge too quickly. Without Judy, Bob would never have become Betty's knight in shining armor. Indeed, Judy's assumptions about Betty's love life are central to the movie. But contrary to what the song says, these sisters have… "two different faces, and in tight places they (don't) always think and act as one." While she's not quite as intuitive as she'd like to think she is, no one can fault her unswerving purpose and devotion to her causes. Judy's intentions are good and her devotion is great. Maybe that's why we identify with her in the first place.

Devotion is God's original idea, as well as an innate characteristic of His personality. Why else would the Creator pursue mankind for an intimate relationship, and then sacrifice what was most precious to Him in order to obtain it?

Unlike Judy (and the rest of us), God's devotion is more than good intentions. The perfect combination of omniscience and devotion prevent God from making assumptions and just hoping for the best. According to Isaiah 14:26-27, God says, "I have a plan for the whole earth, for My mighty power reaches throughout the world. The Lord Almighty has spoken, who can change His plan: When His hand moves, who can stop Him?"

Having a propensity for devotion and loyalty shows that you have something in common with your Creator. Learning more about His personality will demonstrate how devoted He is to you. Reading the Psalms is a good place to start.

This Christmas get to know the real reason for the season–Jesus Christ.
He would die for you to get to know Him.

A GREAT QUOTE FROM
WHITE CHRISTMAS

"There were never such devoted sisters."

A GREAT QUOTE FROM GOD
REGARDING HIS DEVOTION TO YOU

"For the eyes of the Lord run to and fro throughout the whole earth to show himself strong on behalf of those whose heart is loyal to Him."

—2 Chronicles 16:9 NKJV

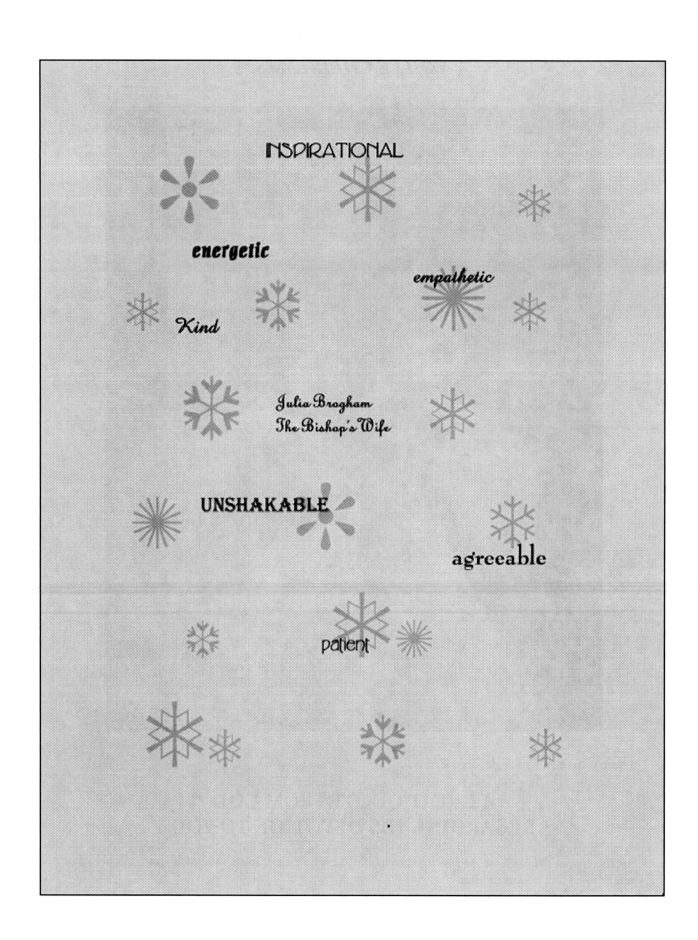

INSPIRATIONAL

energetic

empathetic

Kind

Julia Brogham
The Bishop's Wife

UNSHAKABLE

agreeable

patient

JULIA BROUGHAM
IN
THE BISHOP'S WIFE

"They're a few people who know the secret of making a Heaven here on earth—you're one of those rare people."

What type of woman would attract the admiration of an angel? If the story has any believability, we see Cary Grant as Dudley (a very charming and committed celestial servant) falling for the Bishop's wife.

Julia Brougham is a gentle, reserved woman who is focused on fulfilling the dreams of others. She is willing to go the extra mile and work behind the scenes in order to pursue the visions of her family. She so values these visions that she tolerates misunderstanding and criticism in order to achieve them. Because she displays the virtues of patience, integrity, empathy and insight, she is a model for inspirational leadership and faith. No wonder Dudley feels right at home.

If you're attracted to this movie, it may be because you aspire to share these characteristics as well. In sharing these characteristics, you're sharing community with your Creator. The Bible reveals God to be gentle, patient, insightful and perceptive. Never one to turn aside from His original vision, God is focused and determined to see His people have a relationship with Him.

This Christmas, get to know the real reason for the season—Jesus Christ.
He would die for you to get to know Him.

THE BEST QUOTES FROM
THE BISHOP'S WIFE

"The World changes, but two things
remain constant—Youth and Beauty."
"There are a few people who know the secret of making a Heaven
here on earth. You're one of those rare people."

THE BEST QUOTES FROM THE BIBLE REGARDING GOD'S CHARACTER

GENTLENESS

"He will feed His flock like a shepherd, and gently lead those who are with young."

—Isaiah 40:11 NKJV

PATIENCE

" [I am] the God of patience and comfort."

—Romans 15:5 NKJV paraphrased

PERCEPTION/INSIGHT

"I the Lord search all hearts and examine secret motives."

—Jeremiah 17:10 NKJV paraphrased

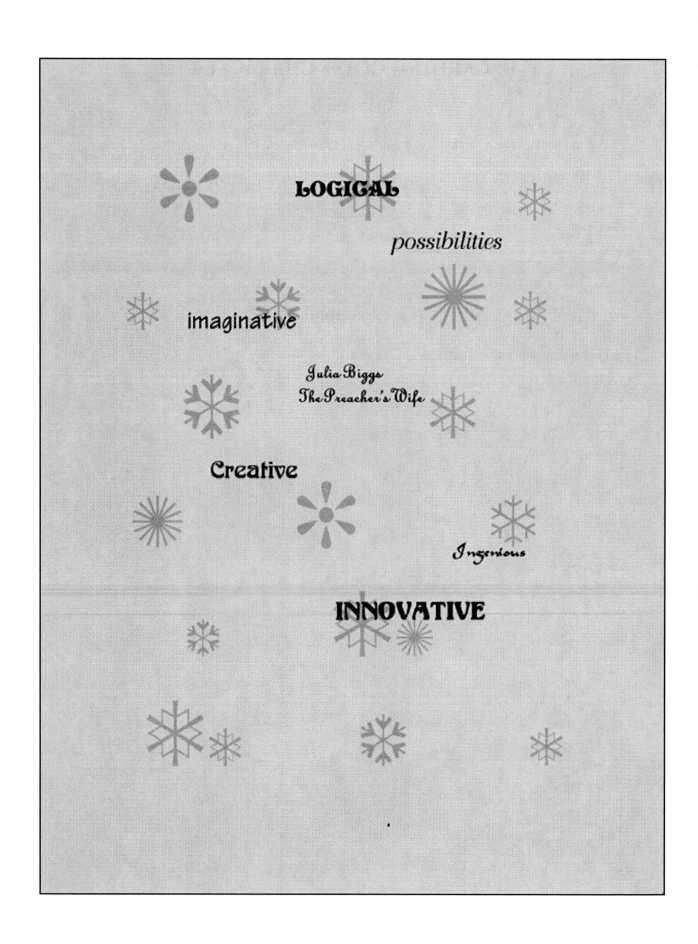

LOGICAL

possibilities

imaginative

Julia Biggs
The Preacher's Wife

Creative

Ingenious

INNOVATIVE

JULIA BIGGS
IN
THE PREACHER'S WIFE

Julia Biggs is the modern version of Julia in *The Bishop's Wife.* Being an Intuitive Thinker (NT), Julia is always setting high standards for herself. She naturally looks at how to improve herself and her surroundings. Creative and imaginative, she has the ability to understand complex issues and the long-range implication of her decisions. Like all NT's, Julia easily imagines possibilities for her husband's church. She also feels a deep obligation to adhere firmly to his original principles, and she won't let him sell out. Julia has no qualms about holding her husband Henry to these same principles. With the supernatural assistance from Dudley, she eventually succeeds in helping Henry achieve his dreams while remaining faithful to the original standards.

If you share the characteristics of creativity plus remaining principled, your personality is probably closest to that of your Creator. While being able to see the possibilities in all of His creation, God Himself is obligated to adhere to his original standards. Those standards are high indeed—holiness, purity and sinlessness. In our human state these are unattainable. Jesus, who is God, arrived on earth in the form of a human in order to be the ultimate sacrifice for humanity's needs. His substitutionary death makes us holy, pure and guiltless.

This Christmas, get to know the real reason for the season–Jesus Christ.
He would die for you to get to know Him.

THE BEST QUOTES FROM
THE PREACHER'S WIFE

"Angels are hardly strangers."
"When we love someone, we are really loving God."

THE BEST QUOTES FROM THE PREACHER'S BOSS

"But God shows His great love for us in that while we were still sinners Christ died for us."
—Romans 5:8 NKJV

Action

This book is intended to be used as a non-threatening means of introducing women to the possibility of a relationship with their Creator. Given this fact, the following ideas are provided as a creative outlet in order to share this book and use it as it was intended. Where applicable, sample fliers and invitations are provided for your use.

Host a CHRISTMAS MOVIE EXCHANGE. Neighborhood ladies are used to the annual cookie exchange, but this idea fosters more camaraderie and relaxation during the busy season. Ask your neighbors to bring their favorite holiday videos or DVDs in order to share the best scenes from the movie. In-home technology makes it possible to cue up to the scenes quickly. Most people love not only to show the clip but also to explain why it's meaningful to their Christmas memories. Don't worry if some of the sample movies aren't represented in the book. There is bound to be one representation of *It's a Wonderful Life* at every gathering. Cover your bases by choosing your own selected movie clip from the book. The ladies can then take the SCREEN TEST and go home with their personalized synopsis of the film which reveals Jesus to be the reason for the season.

LET'S DO SOMETHING DIFFERENT THIS YEAR COME TO A MOVIE EXCHANGE

BRING YOUR FAVORITE HOLIDAY FILMS (DVD OR VHS)

all cued up to the best scenes and quotes

TAKE A SCREEN TEST

to match your personality with those of your favorite leading ladies

CREATE A MEMORY

you'll take home a special souvenir of the evening

We'll get a jump start on our Christmas Spirit
while we get to know each other a little better

I'LL BRING THE COOKIES

DATE:
TIME:

Turn your family room or kitchen into a CHARACTER SPA. Give your neighbors the star treatment by providing the products and equipment for a beauty make-over, self manicure, or pedicure. For those of you who regularly host professional beauty classes or makeovers, create the Christmas spirit by playing the movies in the background and providing an opportunity to take the Screen Test during the treatment. Emphasizing the importance of the eternal as well as the external make-overs will make much more sense in this context.

A "CHARACTER" SPA AND BOUTIQUE
COSMETIC MAKE OVERS
MANICURES
PEDICURES
SPA REFRESHMENTS

TAKE OUR SCREEN TEST TO SEE
WHERE YOU FIT INTO YOUR FAVORITE CHRISTMAS FILMS

DATE:

TIME:

Provide the materials to make simple **MOVIE SOUVENIRS.** We have made lovely and useful mementos of these events by allowing the participants to write memorable quotes on purse mirrors, lipstick cases, and journals. Decorated with sequins and beads, these personalized crafts become a daily reminder of who they are in relationship to their Creator.

Appendix ❧

The following pages are reproducible
if you would like to give them away.

VIOLET BICK
IT'S A WONDERFUL LIFE

"Excuse Me! I think I got a date! But stick around fellas just in case!"

Violet Bick is essential to making Bedford Falls feel like a real place. Every town (every high school, and every office) has someone like her. Flirty, optimistic and determined to have fun, Violet is very busy controlling her own circumstances to ensure that outcome. All of this doesn't preclude her from asking for help when she needs it—and she knows exactly who to go to for that help. Violet is confident enough in George Bailey to know that he won't turn her aside even when her intentions are to use his help for her own purposes yet again.

God will never turn away a genuine seeker. He loves to show Himself faithful to those who need to learn to trust Him. Each time our heavenly Father comes to the rescue, along with appreciation, another logical response should be a little more confidence that God is who He says He is. (He says it all in the Bible. A good place to start is the gospel of John.)

This Christmas get to know the real reason for the season—Jesus Christ.
He would die for you to get to know Him.

DORIS WALKER
MIRACLE ON 34TH STREET

Faith is believing in something when common sense tells you not to.
I believe, I believe—it sounds silly but I believe.

There's not much difference between these two statements uttered by mother and daughter respectively. What these girls needed was proof. It takes until the movie's ultimate scene to finally reveal the evidence which proves that the enigmatic Kris is really Santa Claus. And don't we all feel better knowing our hunch was right?

In our twenty-first century religious smorgasbord, (I'll take a little of this—don't want any of that, it's all good for me, right?"), it may seem silly to believe in the exclusive claims of
Jesus Christ.

But keep believing.

And "add to your faith…knowledge…" because history, geography, archeology, and logic all support the claims of the Bible and its central character Jesus Christ.

This Christmas get to know the real reason for the season—Jesus Christ (through the Bible as well as supporting books like Chuck Colson's *How Now Should We Live* and Josh McDowell's *More Than a Carpenter.* Or simply pose questions to people whose
faith you admire.)

Jesus Christ

He would die for you to get to know Him.

ELIZABETH LANE
CHRISTMAS IN CONNECTICUT

If you think that promises are meant to be kept, then you should spend a little *Christmas in Connecticut* with Elizabeth Lane. Although the movie itself is a lighthearted adventure of mistaken identities, Liz' (two) characters consistently prove themselves to be reliable, agreeable, teachable, and diplomatic. These are some characteristics that God Himself values in order to teach permanent life lessons to those willing to tune into Him.

This Christmas get to know the real reason for the season—Jesus Christ.
He's so anxious to explain how He's kept all of the promises that He made to you.

MARY BAILEY
IT'S A WONDERFUL LIFE

"You see George, you really had a wonderful life."

Perhaps it is more appropriate for our purposes to say,"…you really had a wonderful wife." But George Bailey already knew that. Try as he might, he couldn't resist Mary Hatch. Even though he wanted to "shake off the dust of this crummy little town," deep down he loved the friendly, popular, nostalgic girl who admired him and wanted to go out of her way to provide for him a home.

When someone admires those traits of loyalty, sympathy, graciousness, and idealism in others it is likely that they find a bit of those characteristics within themselves. It's no coincidence that you share these positive qualities or admire their presence in Mary Bailey. Your own Creator designed you with these traits because He is
Loyal
Sympathetic and empathetic
Gracious and

Idealistic Himself. (Among many other wonderful things.)

This Christmas get to know the real reason for the season—Jesus Christ.
He would die for you to get to know Him better.

BETTY HAINES
WHITE CHRISTMAS

When you can't sleep, do you count your blessings instead of sheep? If so, you might identify with that realistic, common sense sister—Betty Haines.

The girl with the "deep-blue" eyes is trustworthy, and idealistic. Having the ability to listen more often than talk, she also prioritizes speaking the truth when she does decide to open up. Although usually calm under all circumstances, she feels strong emotion in response to the drama in her friends' and her own life.

Now we're not fooling ourselves. We know everything's not "wonderful in Vermont this time of year." Betty has some faults (just like all of us) that get her into trouble. But because we're just talking about the positive qualities here, let's examine those for a minute.

It's not just chance that you share these positive qualities or admire their presence in Betty and others. Your own Creator designed you with these characteristics because He is
Trustworthy
Idealistic
Truthful and

Emotional Himself. (Among other wonderful things.)

This Christmas get to know the real reason for the season—Jesus Christ
He would die for you to get to know Him better.

JUDY HAINES
WHITE CHRISTMAS

Among many things, Judy Haines is a devoted sister. She admittedly plays all the angles to promote, first, her sister act and later her sister's future happiness. All through the movie we watch as Judy listens closely to unspoken messages, the wheels in her head constantly turning as she adds two and two…only to get five. Now before we judge too quickly, without Judy, Bob would never have become Betty's knight in shining armor. Indeed Judy's assumptions about Betty's love life are central to the movie. While she's not quite as intuitive as she'd like to think she is, no one can fault her on her unswerving purpose and devotion to her causes. Judy's intentions are good and her devotion is great. Maybe that's why we identify with her in the first place.

Devotion is God's original idea as well as an innate characteristic of His personality. Why else would the Creator pursue mankind for an intimate relationship, and then sacrifice what was most precious to Him in order to obtain it?

But unlike Judy (and the rest of us,) God's devotion is more than good intentions. The perfect combination of omniscience and devotion prevent God from making assumptions and just hoping for the best. According to Isaiah 14:26-27, God says, " I have a plan for the whole earth, for My mighty power reaches throughout the world. The Lord Almighty has spoken, who can change His plan; when His hand moves, who can stop Him?"

Having a propensity for devotion and loyalty shows that you have something in common with your Creator. Learning more about His personality will demonstrate how devoted He is to you. Reading the Psalms is a good place to start.

This Christmas get to know the real reason for the season—Jesus Christ.
He would die for you to get to know Him.

JULIA BROUGHAM
THE BISHOP'S WIFE

"They're a few people who know the secret of making a Heaven here one earth—you're one of those rare people."

What type of woman would attract the admiration of an angel? If the story has any believability, we see Cary Grant as Dudley, (a very charming but committed celestial servant) falling for *The Bishop's Wife*. Julia Brougham is a gentle and reserved woman who is focused on fulfilling the dreams of others. She is willing to go the extra mile and work behind the scenes in order to pursue the visions of her friends and family. She so values these visions that she tolerates misunderstanding and criticism in order to achieve them. Because she displays the virtues of patience, integrity, empathy, and insight, she is a model for inspirational leadership and insatiable faith. No wonder Dudley feels right at home.

If you're attracted to this movie it may be because you aspire to share these characteristics as well. When you share these characteristics you're sharing community with your Creator. The Bible reveals God to be gentle, patient, insightful, and perceptive Himself. Never one to turn aside from His vision, God is focused and determined to see His people have a relationship with Him.

This Christmas get to know the real reason for the season—Jesus Christ.
He'd die for you to get to know Him.

JULIA BIGGS
THE PREACHER'S WIFE

Julia Biggs is the modern version of Julia in this re-make of *The Bishop's Wife.* Being an Intuitive Thinker, Julia is always setting high standards for herself. She naturally looks at how to improve herself and her surroundings. Creativity and imagination fuel her ability to understand complex issues and the long range implications of decisions.

Like all intuitive thinkers, Julia easily imagines possibilities for her husband's church, but she feels a deep obligation to adhere firmly to his original principles and standards. Even when he is willing to overlook them. Julia also has no qualms about holding her husband, Henry, to these same principles as well, and with some supernatural assistance from Dudley, she eventually succeeds in helping Henry achieve his dreams while remaining faithful to those original standards.

Having the creative plus principled tendencies associated with the intuitive thinker, your personality is probably closest to that of your Creator's. While being able to see the possibilities in all of His creation, God Himself is obligated to adhere to His original standards. Those standards are high indeed: Holiness, Purity, and Sinlessness. These are unattainable in our human state. Jesus who is God arrived on earth in the form of a human in order to be the ultimate sacrifice for humanity. His substitutionary death makes us holy, pure and guiltless.

This Christmas get to know the real reason for the season—Jesus Christ.

He'd die for you to get to know Him.

Lightning Source UK Ltd.
Milton Keynes UK
UKOW041004111211

183590UK00001B/2/A